Titles in this Series

Adventures of Richard Wagner
Edward MacDowell and His Cabin in the Pines
Frederic Chopin, Son of Poland, Early Years
Frederic Chopin, Son of Poland, Later Years
Franz Schubert and His Merry Friends
Handel at the Court of Kings
Joseph Haydn, The Merry Little Peasant
Ludwig Beethoven and the Chiming Tower Bells
Mozart, The Wonder Boy
Paganini, Master of Strings
Peter Tchaikovsky and the Nutcracker Ballet
Robert Schumann and Mascot Ziff
Sebastian Bach, The Boy from Thuringia
Stephen Foster and His Little Dog Tray
The Story of Peter Tchaikovsky
The Young Brahms

Frederic Chopin

Son of Poland
Early Years

by OPAL WHEELER
ILLUSTRATED BY CHRISTINE PRICE

Frederic Chopin, Son of Poland, Early Years
Written by Opal Wheeler

FREDERIC CHOPIN: SON OF POLAND, EARLY YEARS written by Opal Wheeler and illustrated by Christine Price. Copyright © 1948 by E.P. Dutton & Co., Inc. Copyright renewed © 1976 by Opal Wheeler. Published by arrangement with Dutton Children's Books, a division of Penguin Young Readers Group, a member of Penguin Group (USA) Inc.

All rights reserved. This book may not be reproduced, stored in a retrieval system, or transmitted in any form or by any means, except for brief quotations in printed reviews, without the prior written consent of Zeezok Publishing.

Reproduction for any use is strictly forbidden.

ISBN 978-1-933573-11-3
Published March, 2007
Printed in the United States of America

Zeezok Publishing, LLC
PO Box 1960 • Elyria, OH 44036
info@Zeezok.com • 1-800-749-1681

www.Zeezok.com

FREDERIC CHOPIN

Son of Poland
Early Years

MUSIC

Mazurka	93
Mazurka	98
Waltz	103
Mazurka	108
Prelude	117
Prelude	120
Theme	130
Grand Waltz	153

CHAPTER ONE

A BLUSTERY WINTER'S night was sweeping an icy cloak toward the wide frozen plains of far away Poland, soon to wrap them in long chilling sleep.

Nowhere, in all that snowbound land, stretching far into the brooding dusk, was there even a breath of spring.

But long captive peasant folk in poorly built huts and cottages dotting the barren countryside, were already bravely dreaming of better days ahead.

"There's food aplenty under those snow banks," rumbled Farmer Pavel, peering through a frostbitten crack in his simple dwelling on the edge of the village of Zelazowa Wola. "A fine crop of winter wheat is sending up strong, green shoots this very minute. And no better soil to grow in, the world over."

His neighbor helper sniffed the wintry air and pulled on stout leather boots.

"Better be showing soon, or there'll be nary a bite for the master's cattle and not a drop of milk for the young ones at the palace."

"Patience, my good man — there's an end to all winters," cautioned Pavel, chief caretaker of Count Skarbek, lord and ruler of peoples and lands for miles around.

Uneasily Pavel watched the last red sun rays light the village windows with tongues of fire. Soon now, with the lengthening shadows, stray wolves would be on the march, stalking unguarded farmyards for a nice fat goose or suckling pig for midnight feasting.

"Time to be finishing chores and locking barns," he growled in deep bass voice.

Tying their heads in bright woolen scarves, the children scrambling to help, the hard working men strode into the gray twilight. Quietly they gazed toward the meadows where the fine palace of their master lay slumbering in soft white snow mantle.

"There's news of a young one just arrived for the Count's tutor," announced Pavel, slapping his arms briskly to keep them warm. "Over yonder in the palace cottage."

"For Schoolmaster Chopin! Tsch, tsch, tsch!" clucked his neighbor in surprise. "A bad time of year to keep new ones alive."

It was true. In the low, three-room cottage, almost buried in whirling drifts, Nicolas Chopin bent anxiously over the

rude cradle of his frail new son and drew it closer to the blazing hearth to keep the baby from the icy breath of winter.

"See that no sparks come near the little brother, my good maiden," he cautioned the three-year-old Louise at his side. "And take good care of the tiny creature while I am away."

Pulling on his sheep-lined coat, he smiled down at the small nurse, so like a proud little mother with gay kerchief drawn snugly over her narrow shoulders as tenderly she rocked the cradle in the fire glow.

"I will sing him Polish songs," she whispered, her dark eyes shining. "And Mother can listen, too."

The gentle crooning, telling of the days when the people of the land were free, followed him as Nicolas went out into the snowy February night.

Over at the palace, just a stone's throw away, he found the Countess Skarbek in her favorite satin chair, reading aloud to her children by the light of the glittering crystal chandelier.

"How now, my good Nicolas," she queried. "What brings you out again on such a night as this? Surely the little one is safe?"

"Ah, yes, safe for the moment," answered her slender, handsome tutor. "But his mother could not rest until I had come to ask a great favor. Justine and I would be pleased if you would grant us permission to name the child after your own son."

Countess Skarbek tapped her richly slippered foot on the rug and sighed.

"Ah, my lovely Justine," she murmured, "there is nothing that I would not do to gladden her heart. How I have missed her since you took her from my house to be your bride! No woman ever had a better lady-in-waiting than I."

She paused a moment in thought.

"Yes, yes, the child," she went on. "Frederic Chopin. A good name, Nicolas. And the christening?"

A shadow passed over the face of her tutor.

"As to that I cannot say, Your Highness. We are struggling to keep the spark of life going."

"Courage, my good Nicolas. There is plenty of time for christening," comforted the kindhearted Countess, taking up her book again.

But sounds of music sent the children scurrying to the window.

"Two violins and a horn!" they announced. "And the players are on horseback!"

"Another invitation to a wedding," laughed their mother. "Neighbors of my faithful Pavel. But the music should bring luck to the little Frederic. Take him my blessing, good Nicolas."

Hurrying back to the three-room cottage, so homelike with its snowy curtains and rows of red geraniums at the windows, Nicolas stole to the back of the house where Justine lay resting on her couch, long fair braids encircling her lovely face.

"Ah, the songs of Poland!" she cried, her cornflower blue eyes bright with tears. "There is nothing in all the world so beautiful. Go quickly, my Nicolas, and invite the players for soup and cakes."

In true Polish fashion, Nicolas greeted the musicians at the low doorway, hand raised in salute.

"Praised be Jesus Christ."

"Forever and ever, Amen," came the fervent reply.

The musicians, gay in special invitation costume of high white hats bedecked with flowers, and with brightly colored ribbons flowing from the left shoulder, stole to the sheltered oaken cradle to gaze solemnly down at the sleeping child.

"A little melody, gentlemen," begged Nicolas quietly.

"It is said to bring him good fortune."

Very softly, at the far end of the room, the players began an old song of country:

> "She shall not die, brave Poland,
> Arise, ye sons, and set her free."

Sad and haunting, the melody crept to the next room where Justine listened hungrily, a prayer moving in her heart.

"Pray God our little one will grow strong and brave," she murmured, "that one day he may take his place beside his countrymen, to fight for the freedom of his native land."

Into the great black pot, swinging on its hook in the yawning hearth, the little serving maid dipped her ladle into the bubbling cabbage soup, bringing speedy warm strength to the grateful neighbor folk.

Small Louise, her long red skirt bouncing merrily, proudly served poppy seed cakes, saving out the largest and thickest for her own.

Anxious weeks crept slowly by, and it was not until the ice melted in the River Utrata and the storks had begun to nest in the tall chestnuts over the door, that Justine folded the delicate baby in a long satin pillow. With Nicolas beside her, she stepped proudly into the crisp April sunshine, radiant with spring.

To the old stone church of Brochau, so like a fortress with its walls and towers, went the happy parents and, standing in a little pool of afternoon sunshine near the marble font, heard with thankful hearts the christening words echoing over the small head:

"From this day on, thou shalt be called Frederic Francois Chopin."

"God be thanked that the little one has been spared to us," sighed Justine as they made their way home through the market place, alive now with rousing country fair.

"And with our little family growing, I shall have to find more work," added Nicolas solemnly.

And so it was, that in the golden days of October, Schoolmaster Chopin moved his dear ones to the sprawling old city of Warsaw, where he would teach French to the students at the Lyceum.

"And best of all, we are still in the country," cried Justine, looking out on the lovely wide park just at the edge of the city.

"Trees and birds and flowers to your heart's content, my fair little wife," answered Nicolas gently. "And a good place for the little ones to grow in the sun."

The bright years slipped happily by, bringing Frederic two new sisters, Isobel and Emily, to keep him good company. And a much larger house they were living in now, with Nicolas teaching the sons of noble families in a part of his own home.

Mischievous, four-year-old Frederic was as happy as a small boy could be, everyone in the household giving him loving attention all of his waking hours.

The time that he loved best was in the early evening, after the supper was finished, when he was allowed to listen with the boys of the school to the lively waltzes and mazurkas played by Justine, Nicolas sometimes accompanying her on his violin or his long, black flute.

One fine evening in spring, Frederic stood beside his mother, his soft brown eyes round with delight as he watched the boys dancing about the large ballroom to the gay melodies of their loved *Pani* Chopin.

The dance finished, the young students gathered around her, clamoring for more music. At once her fine, clear voice rang out through the dusk in what she loved more than anything else, the legends in song of old Poland.

But at the first strain of the haunting songs of the river folk, Frederic broke into such a storm of weeping that Mother Chopin was alarmed, indeed.

"Fritzchen, are you ill, little one?" she cried, brushing back his fair, silken hair.

But the sobbing only grew louder and no one could comfort him.

"Could it be that the child does not like music, after all?" asked Justine, her lovely face troubled at the thought.

"We shall see," answered Nicolas, taking the small boy on his knee. Putting the long, black pipe into his moist hands, he urged gently, "Blow lightly, little one, and see if the flute will sing to you."

But the weeping did not stop.

"Perhaps he would like to try the piano," coaxed his mother, lifting him to the high bench.

As if by magic the tears were ended, and carefully pushing down the keys, Frederic picked out a little waltz that his mother had just played, to the astonishment of everyone gathered around him.

"Frederic! It is lovely," cried Mother Chopin in keen delight. Planning quickly she went on. "You, my dear Louise, must begin at once to show your brother how to play the pieces that I have taught you. And now to bed, my pigeons all, and the first one asleep shall have a fine surprise at sunup."

The very next day the lessons began, and solemnly Frederic sat beside his older sister, learning the music so easily that soon he was making up little tunes of his own and playing them for the boys and the visitors who came to the beautiful Chopin home.

Besides music, there were lessons in reading with his mother. And in a very short time he was reciting long prayers,

and Justine was proud, indeed, as he knelt beside her in the church on Sunday, repeating with her the difficult service by heart.

Carefully she watched over her small son, wondering in her heart what he would be some day.

One night, long after the dancing music was ended, and everyone was in bed and asleep for the night, sounds from downstairs wakened the servant overhead.

Quietly she left her bed and, peering over the banisters, hurried back to the room of her mistress.

"It's the littlest one, Madame," she whispered. "He is down there, playing all by himself."

Together they crept down the stairs, and there, in the darkness, sat the small musician in long white gown, his head bent over the keys as carefully he picked out a mazurka that his mother had just been playing.

"Fritzchen," said Justine quietly, "why do you make music at this hour of the night, small one?"

Slowly the little player raised his head.

"You see, Mother," he answered, "I must practice hard, so that I can take your place and play for the boys when your hands are tired."

Of all the seasons, Christmas was the gayest time of the year for the Chopins, and Frederic could scarcely wait for the festival days to arrive.

There were large parties in the drawing room where lords and ladies and poets and statesmen moved about in rich silk and velvet costume, jeweled swords clinking as gentlemen bowed to fair ladies.

Frederic, buttoned tightly in his best coat with stiff white collar, sat with his sisters on small, straight chairs, watching the procession drifting by. How proud he was of his own beautiful mother, moving like a queen among her guests!

But now it was time for music, and at a sign from Justine, Frederic walked quietly to the piano and, bowing as his mother had taught him, announced in clear tones: "Ladies and gentlemen, I will play for you a Minuet by Mozart."

Not at all frightened by the sea of faces, he began the sprightly music, so dear to his heart, and ended the piece with a flourish amid a round of applause.

And then from across the room came his mother's gentle voice. "Fritzchen, perhaps the guests would like to hear your own Mazurka."

Again Frederic sat at the piano and a jolly dance melody sang out in such rollicking measure that in a moment the guests were tapping their feet in time to the catching rhythm.

"Bravo, little musician!" rang the cry; and, "Justine, this boy has rare gifts! Nicolas, why have you not told us of the child's power in music?" echoed around the room.

But Frederic was not to be spoiled by all the praise and was hurried off to bed with his sisters, to be ready for the festivities of the following day.

And what a day it turned out to be, with mysterious preparations going on in all parts of the house from morning until evening. And at dinner time, just after the Christmas star had begun to glow in the heavens, the doors of the dining room were thrown open and Frederic cried out at the maze of light from the candles, glowing in every part of the long room.

"Enter, my dear ones, for the Christmas feast," invited Nicolas cheerily.

Frederic took his place at the groaning table, feeling cautiously for the layer of straw beneath the white cloth.

"It's here!" he whispered to Louise, his eyes shining in the candlelight.

"Do not touch it, little brother," she cautioned. "Listen, and Father will bless it for the manger scene in the morning."

Solemnly Nicolas rose at the head of the table and, taking a thin white wafer of holy Christmas bread, bit off a little piece and passed it to each member of the family, who ate a morsel in silence.

"We thank Thee, Lord, for this token of Thy Christmas love," said Father Chopin with bowed head. Touching lightly the spears beneath the cloth, he went on: "And we pray for Thy blessing on the manger crèche of the morrow."

"Amen," said Frederic with the others, and the holy moments were over.

This special feast began with steaming almond soup, but by the time the eleventh course came, of sweet currant jelly spread thickly between the layers of poppy seed cakes, Frederic could not eat his favorite dessert.

"You will be hungrier when tomorrow comes," laughed his mother. "Come now, children, the Star Man will soon be here."

Frederic jumped from his chair as if by magic and, scurrying to the piano, tried out his pieces before the kindly saint should arrive to hear them. They must be perfect, or no surprise in store.

There was a noise at the door, and in bounded the Star Man in bright red coat and hat, chuckling merrily through his long, white beard.

"Mer—ry Christmas!" he called cheerily, shaking hands with each of the children and seating himself comfortably in an armchair. "Now then, for the music and stories that I have been waiting a whole year to hear."

Frederic's heart beat faster as he sat to play his pieces. If the Star Man was pleased, there would be a fine reward, indeed.

The good saint nodded and smiled and tapped his foot in time to the music, clapping heartily when it was finished.

"You have been working well, little man, since last I saw you," said he. "Tell me now, where did you find those fine new pieces?"

A look of surprise widened Frederic's eyes.

"Nowhere, sir," he answered brightly. "They just fell out of my head."

"So!" exclaimed the Star Man, beaming. "See that there are plenty of new ones for next year. Now for the surprise."

Loud cries and rollicking laughter echoed through the house as the children raced back to the dining-room doors that had been tightly locked after the dinner was cleared away.

With a turn of the key and a flourish, the merry saint flung them open and there, reaching all the way to the very ceiling was the finest Christmas tree that grew in all the woods around.

Candles were lighted on every bough and with shouts of delight Frederic ran with his sisters to the heaping presents and the mounds of gingerbread cookie men and oranges.

And everywhere, strung on long straws was bright candied fruit, a fair sight to behold.

Parties and festivities lasted for days and six-year-old Frederic was busier than he ever had been, called on to play his pieces at every occasion.

Nicolas, watching closely the boy's rapt expression, became suddenly aware that here was something strange, that even he did not understand. Quietly he leaned toward Justine.

"God is with us in this household, my dear. So much music is here that the boy's heart sings almost to bursting with melody. We must guide him well in the next few years."

"Yes, it is time, Nicolas, for him to work in earnest. He must have the finest teacher possible," agreed Justine, listening proudly to the sparkling music.

To Joseph Elsner, teacher of composition at the Lyceum, went Nicolas to ask his advice.

"Adalbert Zwyny is just the man," said he at once. "A fine musician himself, he will teach the boy well."

And what a strange looking creature Zwyny was, so like a giant, with brightly colored waistcoat and loose-hanging yellow mantle. A gay handkerchief flowed from his pocket as

he appeared at the Chopin door, with a long pencil to keep it company, so thick that Frederic, seated now beside the master at the piano, looked at it curiously.

"The marker — you like it, small one?" growled Zwyny, mopping his red face with a big plaid handkerchief. "But it is not for marking. No, siree! It is to punish lazy fingers that will not do as they are told."

Down went the silken chestnut head, and no one ever worked harder at the long scales and exercises, to the great delight of the master. Here was bright promise, the greatest that he had yet known.

"Listen closely, my Fritzchen, and I will tell you a secret," boomed the great voice beside him. "We will work together so hard that one day you will play as well as the composer whom you admire so much — the great Mozart."

Faster and faster ran the short fingers over the keys until bright red spots burned on young cheeks as Frederic stretched his hands, trying with all his might to please his strict master in the difficult chords and runs.

Never was there any urging to practice. And never was there need of the stout pencil. *Pan* Zwyny shook his great head in amazement as the boy's own compositions tripped from his fingers as easily as a bird sings. But write them down he could not.

"Slowly now, slowly," encouraged his teacher, "and I will put down your melodies in a book for you to keep."

One day when the lesson was over, he spoke quietly to Nicolas and Justine.

"Never have I had such a pupil," he exclaimed. "And each day brings a new wonder. God has given us a great trust, my friends."

"Ah, yes, what you say is true, good Zwyny," sighed Justine. "But the boy is not over strong and should not spend so much time at his music."

Nicolas spoke encouragingly. "Then a good thing it is that the school is closing now, with long weeks for him to roam in the sun. In a few days we leave for our old home in Wola."

The preparations began in earnest, and Frederic could hardly wait for the day to come when his greatest wish would come true, and they would all be on their way to the country that he loved so well.

CHAPTER TWO

MORNING LIGHT WAS stealing through cloudless heavens, sending the stars off to bed when Justine called up the long and silent stairway to the sleeping children.

"Time to leave for the country. Up with you, little ones!"

Frederic bounded from his bed and ran to the window. Such a commotion as there was in front of the house with the wagon being loaded for the journey. Like an elfin creature he darted in and out of the rooms, calling at the top of his voice.

"The country! We're going to the country!"

There was scurrying upstairs and downstairs to get an early start. But at last all was in readiness, and after breakfast, everyone climbed into the carriage and away they wheeled onto the roadway, the heavily laden wagon following close behind.

My, what a day it was, with spring dancing over the countryside. Frederic was never so merry and said so many droll things, and twisted his face into such queer shapes that everyone laughed until they could laugh no more.

Nicolas had been watching the sun, and when it was directly overhead, he nodded his head wisely.

"Time for lunch," he announced amid the lusty cheers of the young travelers.

Picnic food never tasted so good and Justine laughed as Frederic quickly finished his cold duck and asked for more.

"Enough for one time, little rabbit," she cautioned gently. "Now for a bit of walking before we start the last lap of our journey."

Frederic was off in a flash, running through forest and thicket, and long before he knew it, he was far away. In surprise he walked through a giant clump of ferns and found himself in a little patch of peaceful meadow.

The delicate sound of a flute made him stop short and

turning abruptly, he saw to the left of him a sheep herder seated on a rock, piping away on a short piece of willow.

Frederic's heart beat faster and stealing cautiously along, not to disturb the plaintive sound, he drank in the tender melody, so simple yet so beautiful.

But now the sheep had begun to wander, and striding after them, the ragged, large-hatted herder went his way, piping his own yearning song of the fields and brooks and forests of Poland that he loved so well.

Keeping well behind him, Frederic followed quietly, breathing quickly as his ears caught every little change in the tune. But the herder was going faster now, and in a few moments was lost from sight in the deep grasses below the hill.

Listening intently, Frederic followed the thin piping until it was swept away in a little wind that carried the sound far from his hearing.

Suddenly he stood still, remembering. They would be waiting for him at the carriage! Turning quickly toward the forest, he ran as fast as his legs could carry him, calling as he winged through the tall, silent wood.

"Mother! Father! I'm coming!"

This way and that way he darted along, but no roadway opened before him. He must have gone farther than he thought. Out into the deep grasses and on through brambles and thicket he tore, calling at every turn, "Mother! Father! I'm here!"

But there was no answer. And now a strange fear clutched at him. He was lost.

Too weary to go on, with throat dry and aching, and legs cut and bleeding from prickly thorns and underbrush, he fell under a tree, a torrent of sobs shaking his slender body.

The tears finished at last, he fell into a deep slumber, dreaming of following the herder into a strange land. And there were red-coated sheep men piping on every little hill, with hundreds of white, wooly animals dancing about on their hind legs to the loveliest music that he had ever heard.

In the midst of his dreaming he was awakened by shouting near at hand.

"Fritzchen! Fritzchen! Where are you, boy?"

In another moment he opened his eyes to see his father's startled face close above him. Strong arms lifted him gently and carried him to the carriage not far away.

Looking into the anxious faces about him, he began in halting tones to tell his story.

"I followed the shepherd and he was making music on his flute," he explained.

One look at his tear-stained face and bruised body, and there was no scolding from his mother. Quietly she wiped the dirt from his flushed cheeks, and at a nod from his father, the driver started the horses. On they jogged over the countryside and were happy, indeed, to arrive safely at the dear palace cottage.

It was just as they had left it, peaceful and calm, with fires lighted in each of the tall, whitewashed brick stoves, to drive out the spring chill from the three low rooms. The comfortable warmth made them drowsy and soon the children were tucked into their goose-feather beds, with the River Utrata singing them to sleep under their very windows.

What fun there was through the bright summer days, with picnic lunches spread under the wide chestnuts. And there was wading in the shallow stream, where the friendly cows came down to drink, standing knee deep in the fresh, cooling water.

Hunting for birds' nests was a great delight and Frederic's sharp eyes always spied the most, hidden far down in the deep, sweet smelling grasses. And dearly he loved to watch the sweeping fields of flax, so like a slice of heaven as the winds curved them into great waves of misty blue.

Romping and exploring to his heart's content, he was happy as he could be. All but for one thing. He missed his beloved piano at home in Warsaw, with tones so sweet and true as to invite melodies to rush from its keys. The small one in the cottage with its wavering notes upset him and made him very unhappy.

"Why not let the child practice at the palace?" asked Countess Skarbek, visiting with her beloved Justine in the cheery cottage one morning.

"Very well," agreed his mother, adding laughingly, "but you must promise to stop him when you have had enough of his music."

But little did Justine know what pleasure he was to give, not only to the members of the Count's household, but to the many royal friends who crowded around the small musician as he played.

Though he loved the beautiful months in the country, Frederic missed his dear friend, Zwyny, and was glad to get back to Warsaw, to play his new melodies for the good teacher.

"So you have wasted no time, little man!" exclaimed the master, bending over his favorite pupil to listen, amazed, to the bright flow of sound that filled the sunny music room. "Ah, my little Frederic, God has given you a rich blessing," he cried. "But there is hard work ahead, very hard, indeed."

Frederic's brown eyes twinkled merrily.

"But music is not work, *Pan* Zwyny. Music is fun!"

His father's birthday was fast approaching, and locking himself in his room, Frederic labored over his greeting, his big pencil slowly printing the words so close to his heart.

There, it was finished at last! And now for the present. Darting from the house, his swift legs took him to the pastry shop just down the street.

"Bless you this day, young Fritz," welcomed Paul, the smiling baker, pushing his blowsy white hat to the back of his head. "Is it a birthday again?"

"Oh yes, a very special one," cried the young customer, sniffing the good smells and peering longingly at the rows of cakes and tarts. Carefully taking the long-saved coins from his pocket, he held them out in his moist hand.

"Poppy seed cakes," he finally decided. "He likes them the best."

It was hard to wait until evening, but at last, after the guests were seated at the long birthday table, he walked slowly to his father and carefully placed his gift before him. Then, with a deep and solemn bow, he began his little speech.

"Dear Father," said he, clearly and distinctly,

> "How great a joy I feel in my heart,
> That a day so pleasant, so dear and joyous
> Begins, a day that I will greet with the wish
> That long years will pass in happiness,
> In health and vigor, peacefully, successfully.
> May the gifts of heaven fall richly upon you."

"Well, well, my dear Frederic, a finer speech I never heard," declared Nicolas, patting the brown head. "And such a beautiful package, with still another message on top!"

Taking up the paper, he read aloud the printed words.

> "Dear Father, I could express my feelings more easily if they could be put into notes of music. But as the very best concert would not cover my affection for you, dear Father, I must use the simple words of my heart, to lay before you my utmost gratitude and affection."

"Hear! Hear!" cried the guests, saluting the young speaker by tapping their glasses with their spoons until the room rang with the tinkling sounds.

There were many speeches from his friends during the long dinner, but none did Nicolas treasure as much as that of his own son.

But now and then came anxious days for the Chopins, days when Frederic had to be watched over with great care. A thin little body and solemn eyes told that he was not so strong as he might be. Merry laughter and joking would suddenly end, and the piano did not sing as usual. As *Pan* Zwyny saw cheeks become flushed, he quietly closed the piano.

"Come, Fritzchen, you and I will take a little holiday," he would urge gently. "We will see what the world outside has to tell us."

Together they walked through the park and over the meadows, Zwyny telling his young pupil many interesting tales of music and the masters who wrote great compositions. Frederic listened hungrily to every word, happy to be learning so much from his kind teacher.

"Hark you, Frederic," Zwyny interrupted himself, lifting a great finger to his lips. "Hear the song of that goose tender yonder."

There, just ahead, in red-and-blue-striped skirt, her hair tied in gay kerchief, a simple peasant girl watched over her waddling flock, singing the while an old Polish song of work.

"Open your heart to the music of those who toil on the land," said Zwyny. "And store it well in your memory, for in it you will find the life of the people. All of their joys and sorrows they pour into their melodies."

Quietly the master watched over his young charge, coaxing him to sleep under a protecting chestnut, his own yellow cloak spread as a bed to ward off the earth dampness.

Refreshed, Frederic would waken with eyes bright, and relieved, Zwyny listened in amazement as he answered bird calls so truly that the gay, feathered creatures were soon flying over his hiding place, thinking to find their mates.

Through the happy years Frederic studied hard with his teacher until his fame as a pianist spread far beyond his home. And so it was no wonder that on the eve of his ninth birthday, a great honor was to come to him.

"Our noted statesman, Niemcewicz, has sent word that he would be pleased to have our Frederic play at a public concert for the people of Warsaw," announced Nicolas, a happy smile lighting his fine countenance.

At once the household was in an uproar.

"A public concert!" echoed Justine, while the children

clapped and shouted their joy. "And what is the child to play, Nicolas?"

"The famous composer, Gyrowetz, has written a new concerto, and Frederic will play the solo part."

"With an orchestra to accompany him!" exclaimed Louise, looking at her brother with admiring eyes.

While Frederic spent the days learning the new music with Zwyny, Mother Chopin carefully prepared a new costume for the great event.

The special day arrived at last, and everyone gathered around while Justine gently placed the finest lace collar on the handsome new black satin suit. Standing back to view her handiwork, she sighed happily. How like a young nobleman was this child of hers, and how easily he would always take his place in any royal company.

Praises were heaped on his shining, fair head as Frederic stood at the door, ready to leave for the concert with his father.

"Don't forget to bow as Zwyny has taught you! And sit up very straight when you play! Be sure to thank the statesman for this honor that has come to you!" rang the commands behind him.

The large hall was filled with lords and ladies in splendid costume, and as Frederic walked to the piano, warm handclapping followed him.

Before starting the work, he looked at his good friend, Zwyny, seated in the front row in new yellow coat, brighter than ever and, smiling a welcome, straightened his small back and began the difficult composition.

There was rapt attention as Frederic's short fingers flew over the keys, so surely and without a moment's hesitation.

The large audience was entirely forgotten as the small player lost himself in the singing melodies and long, rich chords.

Thundering applause greeted him as he finished the concerto and, not at all upset, Frederic bowed low and took his place beside his father. Above the noise he could hear Zwyny's great voice booming, "Bravo! Bravo!"

"He is a wonder child! Surely another Mozart! We must have him play often!" sounded on all sides.

Calm and happy, Frederic walked home beside his father, to find Justine waiting anxiously for news of the concert.

"Did you play well, my son?" she asked, the moment the door opened. "And did the people like the music?"

Frederic stood still for a moment and then his face lighted in a merry smile.

"Why, Mother, everyone was looking at my collar," said he. "I think they liked it almost as much as I do."

And now invitations came pouring into the Chopin home, and lords and ladies and servants in fine livery came to carry off the young musician to play in the celebrated homes of Warsaw.

But best of all, Frederic liked to see the beautiful horses of the Grand Duke Constantine come prancing down the roadway. Four abreast, with glittering gold and silver harness, their plumed heads were held high, each mounted by a proud cossack in brilliant red coat and high, black fur headdress.

The richly ornamented carriage, bearing the young Prince Paul in costly velvet costume, stopped at the door while a servant delivered the message.

"The Princess Lowika begs that Master Frederic Chopin come to the palace to keep the young Prince company for the day."

With eyes shining, Frederic was soon ready and on his way in the carriage, leaning from the window to watch the high-stepping horses.

On to the massive Belvedere palace they rode in state, peasant folk stopping by the roadside, hats in hand and with heads bowed until the splendid carriage had passed by.

Down the spacious, long drawing room lined with tall gilded mirrors, walked the boys, talking together merrily. And coming to meet them in a shimmering taffeta gown was Paul's mother, the Princess Lowika, known far and wide for her help to the poor. Called the angel of Poland, she was praised throughout the land for her service to those in need.

But a sadder face Frederic had never seen. Perhaps it was because of her fierce and cruel master and husband, the Grand Duke Constantine, who ruled the people with an iron hand.

"You will play for me, good Chopinek," she said in a low voice, her hand on Frederic's shoulder. "Your music will help to lighten the burdens of my heart."

Frederic bowed his fair head and said boldly what he knew to be true.

"You have been kind to our people and I will be happy to play for you, Your Highness."

Instantly a frightened look came over her face and she quickly placed her jeweled fingers on his lips.

"Hush, child! That will forever be a secret between us."

Quietly she led Frederic to the most beautiful piano that he had ever seen. The polished wood was inlaid with bands of shining stones that glistened in radiant colors in the candlelight.

Seating himself on the satin-cushioned chair, Frederic ran his fingers lightly over the keys and his heart beat faster as the rich, mellow tones came back to him. In a moment the air was filled with the brightest and most sparkling melodies of Mozart and Haydn, dancing around the richly tapestried room like magic.

Paul, standing near his friend, smiled happily as his mother's lovely face began to lose some of its sadness. But suddenly all was changed as heavy footsteps were heard, and in strode the stern ruler, Constantine. Scowling angrily, he stood in the center of the room, his gaze fixed on the young pianist.

But Frederic, completely lost in the music, was looking at the ceiling, his hands wandering at will, now, in his own compositions. Like a young angel he seemed, with rapt expression and upturned, soft brown eyes.

Rudely the Duke broke in on his dreaming.

"Young man," he barked curtly, going to the piano, "why do you look up at the ceiling when you play? Are your notes up there?"

Standing at once and bowing in his best style, Frederic gazed at the harsh ruler, unafraid.

"I think better when I do not watch the keys, sir," he explained quietly, and waited for the big man to speak again.

"Well, well," sputtered the Duke, "now let us have something martial. Do you think you could do that out of your head?"

"I will try, sir," answered the young player, his eyes sparkling.

Frederic's bright smile at last found an echo in the stern face above him. After a moment's pause, a gay march startled the listeners, so spirited as to make the Duke nod his head in time to the measure. A pleased smile softened his features, and rapping his big hand against Frederic's small back, he roared his approval.

"Good, child! It is good, I say. I will use it for regiment practice," he barked. "See that you write it down and send it to me at once."

Frederic was elated, and a few days later, with Zwyny's good help, the music was finished and sent off to the palace. Soon it was printed and used for the soldiers to drill, but nowhere was Frederic's name on the composition.

But the young composer did not mind and was proud, indeed, to behold his first composition on printed sheets.

"And now you can see how necessary it is to know how to write down the pieces that you make up so readily," admonished Zwyny. "More time we must spend in learning the rules."

And so there were long hours spent in harmony and composition, besides his lessons in French and Latin and Mathematics and Geography with the boys in his father's school.

Sometimes there were special concerts, when trained musicians came to play or sing for the people of Warsaw. And now there were notices everywhere, telling of the noted Catalani, who would give a concert in the largest hall in the city.

The moment Frederic heard the news, he rushed to his father, begging for permission to hear the great singer.

"But so many florins for a single seat, Fritzchen!" replied Nicolas, finding it too hard to say no to the earnest request.

"Never mind, Father," cried Frederic. "You shall have the money back when I have saved it up for you."

The special evening arrived and, in his best suit, Frederic sat proudly in the great hall and tears of happiness fell on his cheeks unheeded as the glorious tones of the noted singer's voice rolled through the long room. Never again would he hear anything so lovely.

From that night, on through the days, he was in a dream world and could think and talk of nothing but the famous singer, Catalani.

One morning soon afterward, as he was about to go to the upper rooms for his lessons with the boys, a powdered servant in dark red livery appeared at the door.

"My mistress, Princess Radziwill, begs that Master Chopin come at once to her home. The singer, Catalani, is there and desires to hear the young musician play."

All the way to the palace, Frederic felt that his heart was turning somersaults within him. To play for the great artist, Catalani! It was more than he had ever dreamed could happen.

But once in the music room, he was completely at ease at the fine piano with the lovely, kind singer seated beside him in cherry velvet robe, listening in closest attention to the brilliant performance of the young musician.

"Bravo! Bravo!" she cried, throwing her arms around the young performer. "You are a true poet, little man!"

Pouring out her praises in a rush of excited exclamations, she swept around the room, returning to embrace Frederic.

"And now for the pleasure that you have given, Catalani will sing for Frederic Chopin, alone," she ended. "But I will need an accompanist. Could you play for me, my gallant Chopinek?"

"I will try, Madame," responded Frederic bravely.

They started, and not once did the young pianist stumble in the music that he had never heard before.

"You are a born musician, little man," cried the singer, her eyes bright with admiration. "We will hear much of Frederic Chopin in the years ahead."

And when, just two weeks afterward, the liveried servant again appeared at the door with a surprise for Master Chopinek, Frederic's joy could hardly be contained at sight of a beautifully engraved gold watch on a bed of rich blue satin, with the words inscribed on the back in fine lettering:

GIVEN BY MADAME CATALANI TO FREDERIC CHOPIN,
AGED TEN YEARS.

Of all the boys in his father's school, Frederic loved Titus and William and Fontana and Dominik, but of these, Titus was his favorite, to be his friend the rest of his days. What fine times they had together, planning endless jokes and tricks to play on everyone around them.

Often there was sound punishment for their mischief, but no one minded too much, with Frederic to lead them on again.

Above all, they loved to hear him play at the piano, and merry waltzes and mazurkas filled the schoolroom at any time of the day when lessons were at an end.

One evening, when his father was away at the Lyceum, the boys became very unruly, indeed. Quarreling and shouting at the top of their voices, they raced about the rooms, upsetting tables and chairs and making a terrible din until the master, Barcinski, was in despair.

Frederic looked about him in dismay, and rushing to the piano, struck a powerful chord that brought a sudden lull in the confusion.

"Come, everyone!" he commanded. "I will tell you a story!"

Here was new fun, thought the boys. As they gathered about the instrument, Frederic quietly put out the lights and, in the darkness, sat at the piano to illustrate his story.

His fingers stole over the keys in a cat-like walk as he began his tale.

"A fierce band of robbers, in need of booty, stole from their beds in the dead of night. And what a good night it was for plundering, with not a single ray of light from the clouded heavens to betray them.

"Through the black countryside they moved without a sound and, reaching their chosen house, crept softly to the window. All was well. Everyone must be sound asleep."

The cat-like music moved more stealthily over the keys as the boys listened in tense silence.

"Lifting their ladder from a clump of trees where it had lain hidden for their deadly work, the robbers placed it silently against the side of the house, preparing to mount to the window above. But at that very moment a light appeared over their heads and, badly frightened, the robbers ran off at full speed."

Galloping, racing, rushing music flew from the keys of the piano.

"Not once stopping until they reached their lair, the robbers crawled through the small cave opening and, hiding in the dark corners, fell at once into deep slumber."

The tale finished, the music grew more and more soothing until it died away in a whisper.

There was not a sound from the boys, and bending down closely, Frederic discovered them to be fast asleep! Quietly he slipped away and, racing down the stairs to his own quarters, called the family together.

"Come quickly, everyone, and I will show you what a joke I have played on the mischief-makers!" he cried.

In amusement they followed him to the schoolroom and, candles in hand, saw for themselves the result of his storytelling.

At a crashing chord from the piano, the boys sat up in surprise, wondering where they were. But in the peals of laughter that followed, peace and good humor were quickly restored.

Frederic loved his life with the boys at school, filled with mischievous pranks. But far more, he enjoyed the hours with his taskmaster, Zwyny, who was always so patient and kind.

One morning, just after he had reached the proud age of twelve, the faithful master looked at him and sighed. Patting the slender shoulders thoughtfully, he turned to Nicolas and Justine.

"The time has come, my friends. The boy must have a new teacher. He plays as well as I do now and must begin more difficult work. I would suggest the master, Elsner."

Nicolas shook his hand warmly.

"You have taught the boy well, dear Zwyny, and for that we shall ever be grateful."

"And you will always be one of us, you know, master," added

kindly Justine. "Our household would never be complete unless you came to be with us often."

Though he was sad to stop his lessons with his good friend, Frederic knew that he must go on learning, and soon he began the study of composition at the Lyceum with the celebrated Joseph Elsner, who was not only a fine composer of many works, but an excellent violinist and leader of the orchestra in the opera house.

"Ah, a fine boy, sir" said the smiling, round-faced master to Nicolas as he studied his new pupil with keen eyes. "To me he looks like a poet. Yes, I have heard much of this young musician from my good friend, Zwyny. But there is always much to learn. Come, we begin at once."

At the end of the first lesson, Frederic found that there was indeed much more to learn. Over the books of composition he worked with the brilliant master, going over the rules and trying them out in musical exercises, sometimes on paper, and then at the piano in many different ways.

Frederic forgot the time completely and would have played on and on, had not the master stopped him, his gray eyes bright with pleasure at so rare a pupil.

"Slowly, slowly!" he admonished gently. "There is plenty of

time. And remember always to play Bach at home, to see how the great master wrote his music. There is no greater teacher in all the world than Sebastian Bach."

Not forgetting what he had been told, Frederic touched his lips to the master's right shoulder in parting, to be kissed heartily on both cheeks in return and rapped soundly on the back for good measure.

"Fine times we will have together, boy," cried Elsner. "Off with you now, slender legs, to your dinner. You should be as hungry as seven stray wolves."

But hurrying home through the streets of Warsaw, Frederic was soon at his beloved piano, trying out the new exercises. And now that he would have no teacher for the piano, he must go on by himself, learning in his own way.

But one thing troubled him deeply. His hands were too small to reach the chords that he loved to play more than anything else. Something must be done to stretch his fingers farther apart.

Searching through the house, he came upon some small blocks of wood and, tying them between his fingers, went to bed very uncomfortable, indeed, but with the happy thought of what they would do for him.

Every night from then on, he never forgot the blocks and, surely and steadily as the months went on, the fingers stretched farther and farther apart until at last, to his great delight, he found that he could reach longer and still longer chords. His little scheme had worked!

Carefully and patiently he used some of the new rules for writing his compositions. But there were many times when they did not suit him and on he went, writing in his own way the melodies that poured in a stream onto his paper.

A new and long composition was at last finished, and wrapping it carefully, he carried it to the master on his birthday, laying it quietly on the table before him.

"What is this, Frederic?" asked jolly, plump Elsner, untying the long scroll. "Ah, a Polonaise in G-sharp minor, by Frederic Chopin! Well, well, well! Let me hear it at once!"

The master listened, startled, to the composition. In it was the sadness and despair of the poor people of Poland, struggling hopelessly for freedom.

When the young composer stopped playing, there was a fierceness in his face that impressed his teacher deeply.

"Frederic! The music is fine, my boy. I hear in it many things. This I would say to you: always play as you feel, and still more, go on writing as you feel. But above all, remember one thing: great music comes from the hearts of the simple folk."

Frederic's eyes lost their fierceness.

"I will hear much of it now, for tomorrow I go to the country, to stay with my friend Dominik."

"Ah, to Szafarnia. Such a beautiful place, Chopinek. And listen well, to store up melodies for later use."

Happier than he had been for a long time, Frederic raced home, his first new composition under his arm. His master had liked the music!

It would be hard not to write more this very night. But there would be much to do to be ready for an early start in the morning, and smiling happily at the thought, he was soon in the land of dreams.

CHAPTER THREE

IT WAS WELL past midday before Frederic and Dominik got started on their journey, with a carriage wheel to be fixed so that riding over bumpy roads would be safe. Grasping their bundles, they climbed into the rickety conveyance, waving farewell as they jogged off.

"Don't get your feet wet," called Mother Chopin after Frederic as she leaned from the doorway.

"And keep your coat buttoned," admonished Louise, shading her thoughtful eyes from the sun.

"Be sure to write us of all your happenings," cried Isobel and Emily in one breath and laughing at Frederic's pretended tears at leaving them.

Rounding the corner, the boys were away, opening their packages of fruit tarts and cakes and feasting merrily, long before they even thought of being hungry.

"Best have it over with," sighed Frederic, biting into his last poppy seed cake with relish.

The boys leapt in and out of the carriage at every bend in the road, and the driver at last shook his whip at his high-spirited passengers.

"Once more with that jumping and this buggy may refuse to carry you," he reprimanded them sharply.

But little did he know how true his words would be. Scarcely had they gone a half mile when there was a loud, grinding sound and, lurching to one side, the carriage began to topple to the ground.

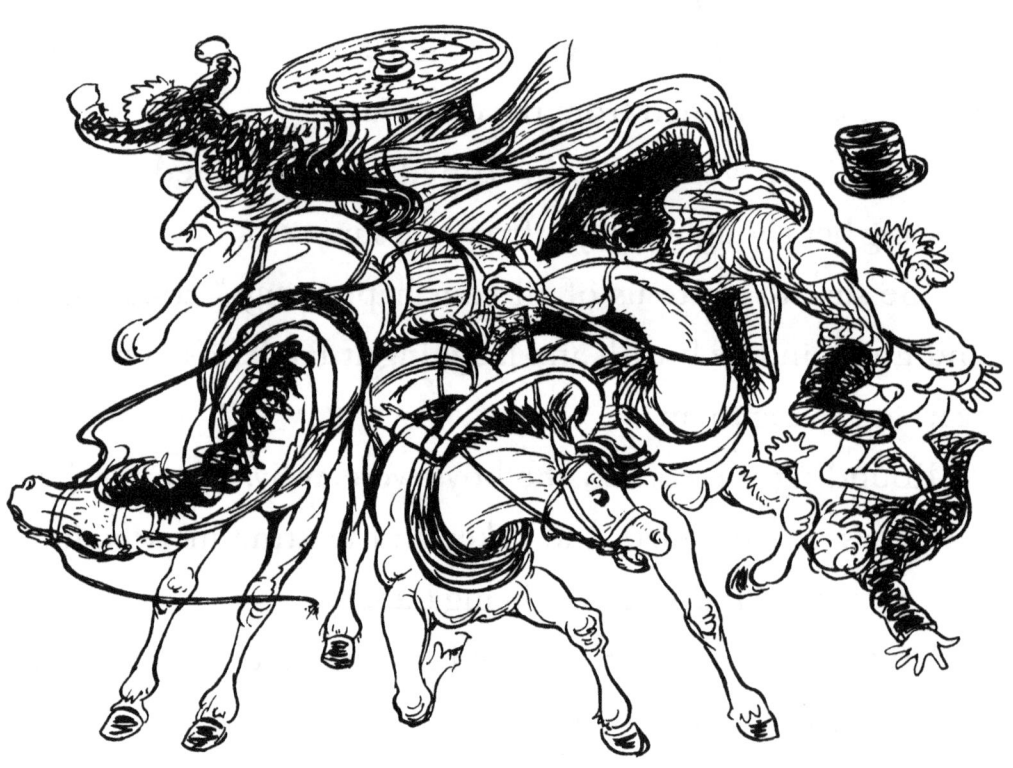

"Jump for your life!" called Frederic. Not a second too soon they leapt to safety, with the top bouncing after them onto the roadway.

Unhurt, the driver picked himself up and steadied the frightened horses.

"Young gentlemen," said he ruefully, "there is nothing to do now but walk the last two miles. Better be using your legs right spry before darkness sets in."

Dusting off their bundles, the boys started out gaily on the last lap of their journey, always ready for fresh adventure. They had not gone far when behind them plodded two lean cows, driven by a sorry looking herder with his feet bound up in old rags.

"A kopek for a ride on your beasts," called Frederic, half in fun.

At the sound of payment, the old man edged along faster, smiling and raising his stick at the boys.

"Yes, yes," he agreed eagerly, holding out his hand for the coin, "I take him now."

Quickly he hid the kopek in his faded blouse, watching the boys closely. "How far you ride him?" he asked, pointing to the animals.

"Two miles," came the answer.

"Two miles? Must be two kopeks," bargained the old man.

With nothing to hold them on, the boys found it a difficult ride. Laughing heartily as the bony creatures moved jerkily beneath them, they sauntered along, calling out encouragingly now and them to their old friend hobbling painfully along behind them.

It was nightfall when they arrived at the beautiful old estate, and bidding good-bye to the herder and putting into the startled man's hand extra kopeks for good luck, they hurried indoors.

After a fine dinner of turnip soup and wild duck and roast pork, topped with pancakes and sour cream, Frederic pleased the household by playing a lovely Mozart sonata. Then, with no urging, the boys were quickly in bed and asleep.

But Frederic was the first one up the next morning, and slipping quietly from the house, was soon busily exploring the out of doors.

The perfume of the freshly cut rye and mint in the fields filled the air and hungrily he sniffed the heady scent. And high overhead and spiraling to earth in such heavenly music as to make his eyes smart, lilting meadow larks were singing their hearts out in the freshness of dewy morning.

The poultry girl was on the pathway now with her lively brood, a song on her lips. Reapers were bending and swaying in the fields of wheat, oats and barley, as they laid flat the waves of shining grain, their deep voices chanting the simplest melody of work.

Frederic, listening with all his might, thought of his father's words:

> "A peasant of Poland will go to the ends of the earth to hear his native songs."

"Fritz! Fritz!" called Dominik, racing over the meadows to find his early rising friend.

But coming upon him suddenly and seeing Frederic's excited face as he bent over his small pocket notebook, he paused until the flow of notes was at an end.

"Come now, Fritz," he begged, "Mother says you have had no breakfast. And I am as hungry as seventeen lion cubs."

Such wonderful days as the boys spent that summer! And Frederic, who must be busy every moment of the day, began to set up a newspaper. He was the editor and the publisher, as well, and articles from his pages he sent home instead of letters.

How his dear ones laughed as they read the carefully hand-printed sheets.

"And there is still more," cried Louise, "listen and I will read it to you."

> "I can now sit a horse and ride where my steed wishes to take me. Clutching its mane, I feel as comfortable as a monkey on a bear's back. The flies select the bridge of my nose for their home, but who cares?
>
> On August 12 a hen went lame, and a drake, fighting with a goose, lost a leg. A cow got so ill that it is grazing in the garden…

On August 14, a decree went forth that, on pain of death, no pig should dare to enter the garden.

The melancholy gobbler, the turkey's brother, got rotten fever from grief and lies without hope of life.

A drake, stealing out of the poultry yard very early one morning, drowned itself."

Of all the places on the estate, Frederic spent most of his time in the peasant cottage of farmer Pavel, listening by the hour as he and his neighbors played on flute and double bass, bagpipe and fiddle, their rich songs of life.

"But tell me, Pavel," questioned Frederic, "how did you learn to play so well on the violin without ever having lessons?"

The sturdy peasant twisted his small cap on his shock of black hair.

"Now where did I learn, you say. And I say to you, nowhere. My father played the flute and the violin before me, and when his hands were too stiff and old with work, he handed me his instruments. 'Play now, melodies to bless my old age,' said he. And so I just played. And so my neighbors just play. That is all."

Frederic looked in amazement at the kindly faces around him.

"But where do you find the music that you play?" he asked.

"It is the same," answered Pavel for the others. "Mother and father sing songs they hear. Sometimes they make up. Sometimes they make neighbor's song longer. When poor people cannot sing, they are very sick."

Borrowing the farmer's flute, Frederic carried it back to the estate and practiced through the week the melodies that he had heard. And when Saturday night arrived, how proud he was to spell old Pavel for the big country dance.

His nimble fingers flew over the stops and the country melodies went on, just as the good farmer had played them, to the great delight of the simple folk dancing merrily around the barn.

When Frederic arrived home, sunburned and happy, his mind so richly stored with the glorious music of the peasants, nothing would do but that he move the piano into his bedroom. Now he could play to his heart's content, and weave into lovely compositions the melodies that he had heard.

Many times in the night an idea would come to him, and lighting a candle, he would hurry to the piano to work at it until it was to his liking and, satisfied, crawl happily back into bed and to sleep.

Through the months and years that flowed by so rapidly, the servants below would waken to hear sorrowful or happy music flying through the air, and would shake their heads.

"Poor young man," they would say. "There is something wrong with his mind."

But his parents and sisters would smile as the heavenly music mingled with their dreams, and because of their love and understanding, they never troubled him.

"Mazurkas, waltzes, polonaises, rush from his pen in a steady flood," exclaimed Justine. "Why, the boy goes to the piano as naturally as to the table."

"Yes, but he plays far more than he eats," laughed Nicolas. "But I am happy that he does not neglect his studies at the Lyceum. Only last week he won a second prize for his excellent work there. And a good thing that he has been doing well at the organ, with the fine surprise that has just come for him. Be quiet, here he is."

"Button your coat," greeted Louise. "And fasten your waistcoat," added Emily. "Be sure to put on your greatcoat when you leave for school," finished Emily, amid rousing laughter.

"My dear children," ejaculated Frederic with a grimace, "without your constant care, I should be a very sick man!"

"But I have news that would quickly make you recover," said his father, smiling. "Elsner has just sent word that you have been appointed organist to the Lyceum!"

There was an outbreak of happy exclamations.

"What an honor, Fritz! You will play for the church services! And we will all come to hear you!"

In a few short weeks Frederic practiced so hard on the organ that he was ready to play any of the church music, and one Sunday morning he took himself through the quiet streets of Warsaw to the chapel of Wiizytek.

Mounting to the organ loft, he slid onto the long bench and began to play as the students entered for the early service.

His classmates for the past year at the Lyceum, they listened with close attention to the new, young organist as his strong solemn music swept through the building.

Now the service began, and Frederic accompanied the solo voice, his feet racing nimbly over the pedals while his fingers found the right keys.

When it was ended, a mischievous gleam came into his eyes. Striking out boldly, he began to make a composition from a melody of the mass that he had just been playing. In a few moments he forgot entirely the soloist, choir and congregation as his strong chords rang through the church, followed by quiet, moving passages and delicate runs and trills.

The leader looked up in consternation. What was happening in the choir loft? But the boys, pleased and delighted at this strange turn of events, left their places in the chapel and gathered around their classmate in enthusiastic listening.

In the midst of the lovely music, a messenger appeared at the choir-loft door, angry, indeed.

"Stop at once," he ordered curtly. "The service must go on!"

Unhappy at leaving the fine concert, the boys filed solemnly back to their places while Frederic went on with the music of the church.

The Chopin household was a very busy one from morning until night. While Mother Chopin went about her many tasks, making everything so cheery and comfortable for her dear family, Louise and Isobel spent their days writing fine books together, and Emily, the youngest, was happiest in making beautiful verses.

Birthdays were always very special events and, now that Nicolas's was fast approaching, Frederic called his younger sister aside for speedy planning.

"Emily, if you and I work hard enough, we might be able to finish the play that we have started, in time for the birthday."

The little sister, his dearest comrade, was delighted.

"We'll write it over again, this time in poetry," she suggested. "And the boys in Father's school can be the actors."

"And we could call it 'The Pretended Rogue,' and it must be comical all the way through," decided Frederic.

At once the task was begun and Emily, already a fine poet, was a great help as the work went on. A short time before the special day, the rehearsals began, and the well-known actor, Piasecki, was called in to help with the last coaching.

But alas, only a few days before the play was to be given, the leading character became quite ill, and there was nothing to do but for Frederic to take his place. Shutting himself away, he worked with a will, determined to know the part well.

The night of the birthday arrived and in a flurry of excitement, the characters donned their costumes. Behind the scenes Emily raced about, helping first one, then another. In a rush of anxiety she tied a velvet cape on her beloved Frederic's right shoulder.

"You won't forget the lines?" she asked nervously, pulling the folds into place.

"Never fear, little sister, but say a long prayer for me," he smiled encouragingly.

The curtains were swept aside and out stepped the players before the large audience. In astonishment, Nicolas and Justine watched closely as the performance went on.

"The Rogue — is it Frederic?" asked Justine, amid peals of laughter at the antics of the chief character.

"It must be," answered Nicolas, "but so completely changed that it is next to impossible to recognize him."

The curtains fell as gales of merriment swept through the audience. At once the celebrated Piasecki hurried to the Chopins.

"Your son is a born actor!" he cried in excited tones. "I should like to find a place for him on the stage at once. How quickly he would make a name for himself in the theater."

"But that is just our difficulty," replied Nicolas quietly. "The boy has too many interests. There is already his piano and organ playing, as well as his composing and writing of stories and poems and plays."

"Yes, and drawing," added Justine, smiling. "Do you know, *Pan* Piasecki, that when Frederic entered the Lyceum, the first thing that he did was to make an ugly portrait of the director, von Linde. His comrades were highly amused, of course. But you can imagine how Frederic felt when he was discovered by von Linde, himself, and the portrait taken from him."

Amid amused laughter, Justine went on.

"But that is not all," she continued. "In a few days the portrait was returned to him, marked 'Excellent.' And you can understand why our son is so fond of the director, and each week goes to his home to play duets with Madame von Linde."

Now that he was the finest pianist in all Warsaw, Frederic was warmly welcomed in drawing rooms everywhere. And when a new instrument, half piano and half harmonium, had been placed with great ceremony under the dome of the largest church in the city, he was pleased, indeed, to be invited to play on it.

"This will be one of the most important occasions in the history of Warsaw, young Chopin," said a pompous gentleman from the council of the city. "The exalted ruler, Alexander the First, will be present at the playing of the new instrument."

Frederic bowed his head at the words.

"I am deeply honored," he replied, trying to still the rapid beating of his heart. "And I will do my best to please him."

Such flurry and excitement as there was in the Chopin home to get Frederic ready for the special event.

"There must be a new coat," declared Justine, "as well as an embroidered waistcoat. And no time to lose in getting them made."

While the planning went on, each day found the young pianist at the church, trying out the new instrument and deciding what music would best be suited to it. And hours

of practicing there must be, to be sure that there would be no mistakes.

All of Warsaw was up early on the special morning and great crowds of people flocked through the streets to find a place where they could see the glittering procession as it would move solemnly on its way through the city.

Frederic, dressed in his fine new clothes, was admired by everyone in the family, and together they made their way through the excited throngs to the church.

Cannons fired a salute, announcing the arrival of the

mighty parade and, at last, into the building it moved in majesty, costumes jeweled and more magnificent than had been seen for long years in the old city of Warsaw.

From his place in the organ loft, Frederic looked down on the brilliant gathering, headed by Alexander, himself, who was seated with ceremony where he could see the new instrument and the player.

At a signal, Frederic turned to the keyboard and, lifting his hands, began the special concert. But now all worry left him, and the fears that he might not play well enough vanished as the music rose and fell in lovely waves of sound.

At last the hour was at an end and, smiling, Alexander led the royal procession from the church. And so pleased was the visiting ruler with the concert, that soon afterward he sent his special messenger to the Chopin home with a small box marked: FREDERIC CHOPIN, MUSICIAN.

"Open it, Fritz! Quickly!" cried his sisters, fluttering around their beloved brother, trying to guess the contents of the beautifully scrolled package.

But they did not dream what a treasure lay hidden in the satin folds lining the box. From a hidden corner, Frederic drew a handsome gold ring, set with a jewel that glistened brilliantly in the sunlight.

"A diamond!" he gasped. "And so large!"

In amazement, Nicolas examined the stone.

"It is truly a kingly gift, my son," he admitted, "and of great value, as well."

Putting the ring on his finger, Frederic strutted around the room amid the laughter of his family.

"Now I am a rich man," he cried, "and as such, I shall take my place as a leading citizen of the land!"

But his thoughts turned quickly enough to his work, for now were to come some of the greatest moments of his lifetime. Two big concerts he would give for the people of the city. And they would be entirely his own, with some of his best compositions at the close of each program.

My, how many hours he spent in practicing, especially a concerto by Moscheles, said to be the hardest piece ever written for the piano. But conquer it he did, and played it with such finish and power that the whole of Warsaw talked of nothing else.

In the days that followed, Frederic made a great decision.

"My life must all be music now," he declared joyously. "Nothing else can compare with it!"

And that same morning, when the first printed copy of his Rondo in C minor, was placed in his hands by his master, Elsner, his happiness knew no bounds.

"With great pride I bring you your dearest treasure, my pupil. It is excellent music, and you may well be happy over this achievement."

And these two compositions that Frederic wrote later, will give you great pleasure.

MAZURKA
(TRACK 1)

MAZURKA
(TRACK 2)

But the excitement of concerts and his feverish work in composing were telling on Frederic. And with his beloved sister, Emily, far from well, Mother Chopin was worried, indeed.

"Why not send them off to the watering place of Reinerz," suggested Nicolas. "A short time there would do them a world of good."

Justine sighed with relief.

"The very thing," she agreed. "I will go with them and take Louise for good company."

The plans were soon completed, the packing quickly done, and the little party set out in high spirits, especially Frederic, who, as usual, filled the riding hours with such fun and merriment that no one minded the journey in the least.

"Here we are!" cried the chief entertainer, helping his mother and Louise and Emily to the ground.

Soon they were comfortably settled and enjoying their new life exceedingly. Frederic and Emily were up every morning at six; and at the fountains, sauntering along with glasses in hand, they drank the curing waters while a little band played music for them.

But far more, they loved the long walks through the beautiful mountains and looking down into the green washed valleys far below. Lying on the sun-warmed rocks, they dreamed together of their years ahead.

"Would that small white house in the meadow yonder do for you, my little queen?" asked Frederic gravely. "There you could write your verses all day long."

Emily, so merry and wise, listened in rapt attention to her adored brother.

"And with a wave of my hand I would command you to refresh me with your music whenever I became weary," she answered happily.

Back to the inn they took themselves at sunset one day, to find their mother and Louise very much upset, indeed.

"The two little children who have been playing around our

door have just lost their dear mother," said Justine sadly. "And now there are no funds to pay for their passage home."

Frederic's dismay quickly turned to relief as a means to a way out formed itself in his mind. At once he hurried off to find the innkeeper.

"I am in need of a piano, sir," said he. "If you could find me one at once, I should be grateful."

The sleepy little man drew his eyebrows together in thought.

"A piano, you say? Well now, if you take good care of it, you might use the new one in the hall."

A new piano! This was luck, indeed! Frederic hastened at once to the low building and shutting himself in, worked at top speed until in a very short time he was ready to give a concert.

Straightway the word went round and, rallying to his call, the patients of Reinerz gathered under the peace of the starry heavens that evening at the little cure house, paying gladly for their tickets at the door.

Mounting the platform, Frederic took his place at the piano and the audience listened entranced to the music of the young artist from Warsaw.

And this little waltz that Frederic wrote, you will surely want to play.

WALTZ
(TRACK 3)

When the concert was over at last, Frederic watched jubilantly as the money was counted. Now there was plenty to send the children home, with a goodly sum, besides, to take with them, thanks to the kind heart of the young Warsaw musician.

Happily at home again, Frederic went at once to his master Elsner to tell him of his journey. At the end of their visit, as he was about to leave, his teacher held up his finger, ready to pronounce his usual parting message. But his pupil interrupted him, laughingly.

"I know, master! 'Never forget one thing: Music comes from the hearts of the common people,'" cried Frederic, saluting his teacher on the right shoulder.

"From the hearts of the common people" echoed on in his mind as he passed through the streets. Suddenly he stopped short, an idea in his mind. Smiling brightly, he went straight to the home of his friend, Fontana.

"Jules," said he, his eyes twinkling, "would you like to go on a little expedition?"

Sensing that something unusual was about to take place, Fontana answered readily.

"I am at your service, Mr. Freddie. When do we start?"

"At once. Here, we shall take this coach and arrive at our destination as quickly as possible."

On the way into the country, Frederic unfolded his plan, slipping coins into his friend's hands. At the first little village, the boys jumped from their lumbering conveyance and wandered through the streets. Every lad they met was given the same questioning.

"Can you play on a musical instrument? Then bring it quickly to the public square and you will earn some pieces of silver."

To earn money! This was unheard of, and in a very short time a band of poor country boys was standing on the green before Frederic.

"Now then, lads, we are going to play some music that I will teach you," said the leader. "Listen carefully, and each day when you have finished, go home and practice well, to be ready for the next rehearsal."

What a task lay before him! The young conductor sighed many times through the days, but with Jules to help him, went on with the work. Most of the boys knew nothing at all about the instruments in their hands, but patiently they were taught, with coins to help, until the tones were sweet and true.

And their own melodies, carelessly whistled between work, Frederic wove into charming compositions until the boys smiled with joy at the new parts he made for them to play.

You will want to hear this spirited country dance that Frederic wrote.

MAZURKA
(TRACK 4)

111

At last the day came when the music suited him, and with a pleased smile, Frederic saluted the grinning band.

"We are ready, boys," said he. "Tomorrow we will meet earlier than usual. Be here with your instruments and we will start off together on a little adventure."

CHAPTER FOUR

THE MORNING WAS bright with the promise of early summer as Frederic dressed hastily and slipped quietly from the house. Down the drowsy street he hastened on winged feet, hoping that nothing would upset the plans he had made so carefully.

Under Jules's window he stopped short.

"Fontana! Up with you, boy. It is time that we were off," he called anxiously.

His uneasiness was soon at an end as a bright face appeared around the corner.

"And a very good morning to you, Mr. Freddie," cried Jules, the excitement of the moment in his handsome face.

"Now if the boys are on time, all should go well," responded Frederic.

"But how shall we get them into town?" asked his friend.

"Our wits will have to come to the rescue and help us to find a way. Run, Jules, we must catch that stagecoach or we are lost."

Nimbly the boys swung onto the steps just in time and went rattling from the city out into the lovely fresh countryside.

There, at the side of the roadway were the boys, clutching their instruments and staring at the coach, hoping to see their leader among the few passengers.

"Morning, comrades!" called Frederic as the boys swarmed around him. Then, looking about him quickly, he spied a farmer with an oxcart, lumbering off toward the fields. In a moment he was walking by the team.

"Sir, I am in need of a cart for a few hours," he began. "If you would lend it to me, I will pay you well."

The farmer took off his hat and scratched his head.

"The cart belongs to the master," he explained. "And a full day's work to be done, besides."

"But look you, my good man," urged Frederic, "it will be for a very short time. And I will pay you double the amount."

At sight of the handful of silver coins, the man climbed down and in the next few moments the boys were standing in the cart and lumbering off toward the city of Warsaw.

Back at the Lyceum, the final music program of the year was well under way. And a very special time it was, too, with visitors on hand for the performance. In the audience sat the Chopin family, waiting for the moment when Frederic would

appear. It was his last year at the Lyceum and they wanted him to play well, indeed.

It was almost time now for the last student, and *Pan* Elsner looked carefully around the room. How glad he was that he had saved the best musician until the end. But where was his favorite pupil? He had not seen him all that morning.

His worry grew by the minute and turned to despair as the young pianist on the stage finished his selection and left the platform.

Suddenly from the back of the room came the sound of shuffling bare feet mingled with muffled laughter. Poor Joseph Elsner held his head in his hands. That Chopin boy! What mischief was he up to now?

Onto the stage Frederic led his ruffian band of country peasant boys, with hair and clothes unkempt and frightened eyes looking out from unwashed faces.

"Steady, boys!" commanded Frederic quietly. "Ready now. All eyes on me!"

At his signal, the music began and a flood of glowing, joyous melody poured from their battered instruments, music from the countryside woven into the loveliest compositions by their leader. Mazurkas, the spirited country dances, so dear to the heart of the Polish people, floated through the hall until the audience was lost in their beauty and bright rhythm.

Then, standing at attention, the boys listened while their leader sat at the piano to play the new composition that had been growing in his mind for the last few weeks.

The glory of the Polish countryside unfolded, of sunlit fields with larks soaring overhead, of the Wisla rumbling through the meadows, of calm and mighty forests and of peasants resting in the shade of the pear trees.

PRELUDE
(TRACK 5)

And wondering, Elsner sat listening intently. His pupil had indeed proved that great music comes from the heart of the simple folk. Surely Poland would never be forgotten with this boy's melodies to keep the memories alive.

"He is a genius," he found himself saying over and over. "I am proud to have spent these years with him."

But now came one of the darkest times that Frederic was ever to know. His beloved comrade, Emily, was very ill, indeed, and all noises in the house were stilled. Through the anxious nights and days, Frederic crept to her bedside to hear the same request.

"Play, Fritzchen. Play your beautiful music for me."

The gentle strains floated down to give her comfort as through the night hours, Frederic played the melodies that she loved best. But one day she slipped away to a far country, never to return.

This lovely prelude of Frederic's you will want to hear over and over again.

PRELUDE
(TRACK 6)

Frederic could not believe the dreadful news and took himself off to the schoolroom, where no one would see his weeping for the dearest friend who had left him. Through the days and weeks he could not be comforted, and in despair, his parents sent him off to the country to be with his devoted Titus.

It was not until Frederic began to play and compose again that his dear friend knew that his heart was getting well. Back home he went, but the memories were so sharp that not even the printing of his Mazurkas made him happy. Justine and Nicolas were worried, indeed.

"Why not send him to Berlin with our friend, Jarocki, who must attend a meeting there?" suggested his father.

"The very thing," exclaimed Justine in relief. "I am sure that Fritz would be no trouble to him."

Frederic was overjoyed at the idea and at once sent off word to his friend in the country: "Dear Titus, I am writing in a half crazy state and hardly know what is happening to me, for I am starting for Berlin!"

But the doctor, shaking his head over the excited young man, gave his warning.

"A little sightseeing, but very little, mark you. And be very sure that you rest a great deal," said he gravely.

But Frederic kept his secret well. He had already bought tickets to every musical event in Berlin!

On a fine September morning, his pockets filled with silver pieces given him by his parents, Frederic called good-bye to his dear ones and started off in the carriage for six long and hard days of travel.

In and out of the cool, dark forests they rode and on past villages, most of them owned by members of royal families. Poor peasant folk, working out their lives for their masters, stood at the side of the road, hats in hand and heads bowed low as their lords and rulers passed by.

Frederic, watching closely, felt his heart burn within him. Fiercely he turned to the scientist.

"It is wrong to hold these workers of the land as slaves," he cried hotly. "People the world over must be free!"

But the frightened Jarocki laid his hand on his young friend's arm.

"Hush, Frederic, someone will hear you," said he. "The day for freedom will come. But now we must be patient, for there is nothing that we can do to help."

At last they stopped getting in and out of the coach at every tiny place, and with fast-beating heart, Frederic found himself in the great city of Berlin, ready for any adventure.

Through the handsome streets he roamed and, sauntering over the well-built bridges, visited the piano factory, amazing the workers by playing on all the new instruments with fire and power.

"Who is he?" they whispered among themselves. "Surely a great musician is here with us."

Theaters and concerts Frederic visited daily and was overjoyed at hearing the master, Handel's, music. And the well-known composer, Felix Mendelssohn, was at one of the concerts where his own music was being played.

If only he could speak to him! Frederic stole as near the handsome young composer as he dared, listening with all eagerness as he conducted the orchestra in his bright and joyous music.

Each day in his small room, he sent off long letters to his parents and friends, who were happy to hear of the fine times that he was having.

"I am sorry to tell you that our time is up, Fritz," said Dr. Jarocki late one afternoon. "My meetings are over, so we may start back in the morning."

Frederic would have liked more days to ramble in the fine, bustling city. And so he was a little sad to set out in the coach with his friend to begin the long, six-day journey back to Warsaw. Out came the long porcelain pipes of their fellow travelers and the droning talk began.

Soon the air became stifling and coughing violently, Frederic climbed outside with the driver where he could breathe freely again the clear, brisk air.

"Going far, young man?" asked the coachman in a slow drawl from the side of his mouth, pulling his muffler closer around his thick, red neck.

"To Warsaw," answered Frederic, watching the driver's face closely so that he could play the part when he arrived home again.

But instantly he forgot the man when, coming into a deep wood he heard the sound of chopping and singing.

"Stop! Stop!" he cried, and springing from the seat, climbed down like a squirrel and was off through the trees.

Just in sight of the woodcutters he stopped. Sitting by the roadside, he took his faithful little black notebook from his pocket to jot down quickly the notes of the peasant cutter's song with its slow and rhythmic beat in time to the swinging of his ax.

Delighted with his treasure, Frederic hurried back to the roadside, but the coach was nowhere to be seen. They had gone off without him! Dashing along on nimble legs, he came upon it suddenly around a bend in the road, laboring in heavy, deep ruts.

Hastily he climbed aboard and sat again with the driver, who turned on him in anger. "See here, young fellow," he began, but seeing the shining eyes of his seat mate, stopped abruptly, mumbling on in his beard.

But Frederic had not heard. Already in his mind the woodcutter's song had begun to take form in a composition, enriched with long, spinning chords and turns, broken by the short accent of the blow of the ax.

In a low whistle he was making the charming melody, while his fingers worked out passages on his knees.

"So!" broke in the driver, an amused smile covering his bearded face. "You are one of them music makers, eh?"

"Only that," answered Frederic, laughing, "and nothing more."

His bones weary and aching from long hours of lurching and jolting over rough, ill-cared-for roads, Frederic was glad to crawl over the wheels and stand on shaky legs at the door of the inn at Züllichau.

"Now for a fine, hot dinner to save us from starvation, eh, Fritz?" called Dr. Jarocki.

Pushing open the heavy door, he sniffed hungrily the roasting meats on the spits before the fire. "Just time for some good food, and on we go," he announced, searching out the innkeeper to order his dinner.

But Frederic had a far different thought in his mind. Searching quietly through the rooms, he came at last upon a worn and battered piano, but at sight of it his heart sank. How could anyone make music on such an instrument?

Seating himself on an old chair, he ran his hands over the keys, and was startled to find that it was in perfect tune!

"Heaven be praised!" he exclaimed under his breath. In an instant, joyous music filled the inn and from every corner came astonished travelers to listen.

Excited at having such an artist in his dwelling, the giant innkeeper ran in, all out of breath, with his wife and daughter, to enjoy the concert, all three roaring their approval after each number.

An old musician with cherished pipe in his hand, stood a little apart in the shadows, living again his past and dreaming again the days that had been.

The hours rolled by and hungrily Frederic played on, unmindful of everything about him, until suddenly the voice of a servant broke in harshly on the music.

"The horses are ready," he announced bluntly.

In a rage, the keeper turned to the door.

"The wolves take you for a goat!" he roared, and putting his great hands on Frederic's shoulders, pushed him back to the piano.

"My dear fellow, do not stop," he begged earnestly, his wife and daughter echoing his entreaties. "Play on, my brave one, and you shall have fresh horses of my own choosing at any hour of the day or night."

Frederic was only too happy to go on with his music, and when at last his hunger was satisfied, rousing cheers greeted him on all sides. The old musician hobbled to the piano and embraced him heartily.

"If only Mozart had been here," he cried, "he would have grasped your hand and cried 'Bravo!' young man."

Overcome with gratitude, the innkeeper showered every delicacy of the house on his young guest, filling his pockets with sweetmeats and carrying him in his strong arms to the coach.

But a good part of the journey was over, and in a short time now, Frederic was at home again, telling his eager family of his exciting adventures.

"Come, Fritz, we have a little surprise for you," cried Louise and Isobel, taking him by the arms and leading him upstairs to a little room under the roof.

Opening the door, Frederic walked in, and there was his beloved piano and an old bureau, brought especially from his room below.

"My dear children," he cried happily, his arms encircling his kindhearted sisters. "You have made this room for me to work in!"

"It is to be your den, where you can be alone and entertain your friends as often as you like," explained Louise.

How Frederic loved his new workroom where every day now he spent long hours in practicing and composing. And badly he needed new music exercises to strengthen his fingers and make them go even faster, so down he sat to write some for his own use.

The months raced by and music rolled from his pen in a steady stream: sonatas, rondos, polonaises, two waltzes, and Variations on a Theme, which he dedicated to his friend, Titus.

And later it was this very piece that the great master, Schumann, was to discover and in his magazine write about so glowingly, exclaiming, "Hats off, gentlemen, — a genius!"

You may want to try this smooth flowing theme that Frederic composed.

THEME
(TRACK 7)

"Fritz! Fritz! Where are you?" Isobel's anxious voice called through the house and up the quiet stairway one morning.

Leaving his worktable, Frederic opened his door, twisting his face into such a clownish expression as he looked down at the intruder that she broke into peals of laughter.

"Come here at once, you silly fellow," she mocked sternly. "Prince Radziwill has sent his coachman to take you to his estate for a week."

Frederic's face sobered at once in real concern.

"Oh, my child, do run and tell the servant that I cannot go. You see, I could not leave in the middle of a composition."

"Ah, Fritz, do put it away now," begged Isobel. "It will do you good to go, for always you come back so well and happy after you have been with the Prince. See, now — I will help you pack."

Frederic stopped a moment to consider.

"Very well, my fairy goblin," he sighed. "And be sure that you put in eighteen pairs of satin trousers, twelve night robes of purest silk, and my gold headed walking canes. Besides..."

"Stop! Stop! There is all too little time for the packing," laughed Isobel. "But how we shall miss your foolishness when you are away," she added wistfully.

Soon the simple clothing was in the case and Frederic was on his way. Arriving at the fine estate near Poznan, he was warmly greeted by his good friend, Prince Radziwill.

"Ah, my dear Frederic, what a man you have grown to be, since last I saw you," said he, looking searchingly at the noble, slender young man with fine open countenance, his head held high, crowned with silken chestnut hair. "But come, there will just be time for a little music before dinner."

Soon Frederic was ready and, making his way down the broad staircase to the handsome music room, met among the royal visitors, fine musicians from Italy and Germany. How different was their manner of playing, but how melodious their compositions.

"Now Frederic, you and I will play a little duet, yes?" invited Prince Radziwill, tuning his cello at the piano.

The Prince loved music above everything else and played very well, indeed, even composing a little. But above all, he liked to hear Frederic play.

And so the days were filled with glorious music. Sometimes Frederic sat alone with the two princesses, Wanda and Elise, to give them lessons on the piano. And he was amused, and readily gave his consent to the pretty little Elise to make his portrait and, when it was finished, smiled and shook his finger reprovingly.

"But see, my fine young artist, the nose is not nearly long enough. And so you must waste much more paint, poor dear. Here now, let me show you on this extra piece of paper."

Going to a long, gilded mirror, he looked at himself intently, and to the astonishment of both princesses, made an excellent likeness with a few strokes of the brush, and sent them into peals of laughter by adding little animals sliding down his nose.

On the third day, Frederic was delighted to hear the special announcement of the Prince.

"My good friends," said he, "tonight we will dance a polonaise. Please come prepared for the occasion."

Such preparations as there were in the palace that day, with polishing and shining and arranging of flowers in the gardens for startling display! Great lamps were set up to give brilliant light and surprise passageways made everywhere throughout the grounds.

In his room, Frederic chose his finest waistcoat and best satin top coat and breeches and, dressing with great care, joined the large gathering below in the spacious hallway.

With great ceremony, Prince Radziwill sought out the fairest and most highly honored lady among the royal company.

"I beg for your hand in the polonaise, Your Highness," said he, bowing low.

The gentlemen with their ladies formed in long lines behind the handsome couple and, at a signal to Frederic, who was seated at the piano, the procession began with the stately, martial music of measured tread.

In his best uniform, decorated with costly embroidery and with a furred cape hung over his shoulder, the Prince led his guests through the brilliantly lighted gardens, stopping now and then to make a sweeping gesture, the long line of men imitating him in solemn style.

Through the galleries and secret passageways marched the glittering procession, the heavy silk of the ladies' dresses whispering as they walked, the swords of the gentlemen clanking as they bowed to their ladies in proud and gallant manner.

Frederic's music rose and fell in measured rhythm, telling of Poland's great days of victory and of her pride, still, in defeat.

With a fanfare of the trumpets, the long dance was ended, the two young princesses in shimmering satin hurrying to

their father with words of praise for leading the procession so well.

But the Prince was intent on reaching Frederic and, striding to the piano, held out his hand.

"My good friend, where have you found such a glorious polonaise? Never have I heard the history of Poland so proudly displayed in her long years of struggle and defeat."

The young musician, his eyes still brooding over the melodies that he had just played, rose and bowed gravely, hesitating over his answer.

"The music is mine, Your Highness. I composed it as you led the procession," he said simply.

The Prince looked intently into the warm brown eyes.

"It is the finest of your compositions that I have been privileged to hear. Lose no time in setting it down, Frederic. It will bring you honor one day."

Frederic's little attic room was becoming quite a meeting place now, and happily he welcomed his friends to his hideaway. Zwyny and Elsner, who still helped him with problems in composition, came together one evening to the small den and, with Nicolas and Justine, sat to listen to the young artist.

When he had finished playing, there was thoughtful silence. Elsner was the first to speak.

"You are ready to spread your wings now, Frederic."

"Ah yes, master, I have been restless since coming home from Berlin, with a longing to see more of the world. But where would I go?" he asked.

Then a thought flashed into his mind and he cried out in delight.

"My three friends, Celinski, and Hube and Franz are going to Vienna, the city of music!"

"And why not go with them?" finished his father with a smile. "A good idea, Frederic. And you could play for the people of the city and find out if you would like to spend the rest of your life in being a pianist."

But at his words, Frederic was troubled.

"How could anyone wish to hear me in a city that can boast of a Mozart, a Haydn, and a Beethoven?" he asked forlornly.

"Tut! Tut, lad!" admonished Elsner. "Why not, pray? They are no longer there, and always there must be new musicians. And besides, you could call on the rascal, Haslinger, and ask him why he has not published your Sonata and Variations which I have taken such care to send him."

A new determination came to Frederic after listening to his master.

"Perhaps I could play them for the people myself, and let them be known in that way," said he.

"Bravo, Frycek!" cried the jolly little master. "And the sooner, the better."

With the little money that he had, Nicolas sent Frederic on his way one sunny July morning.

"Hooray for Vienna, the City of Gaiety!" cried the happy wanderers as they rolled merrily along."

But to Frederic it was a journey to the land of his dreams. He would walk in the streets where the master music makers had lived: Mozart and Haydn and Schubert and Beethoven, whose works he had studied so long and loved so well.

"Let us not hurry on the way, my friends," cried Hube. "Why not stop and see something of Poland's glories?"

"Bravo!" echoed three lively young men. And when the coach arrived at the ancient capital of Cracow, they leaped out, to walk through the stately corridors of the famous University. On to the castle they tramped, to visit the home of Poland's kings and to talk in low tones of the fair days of the past.

After a week in the historic spot, it was time to go on. With sighs of regret they left the beautiful countryside of Galicia behind them, and nearing Ojcow, were as hungry as four young men could be.

After a hearty Sunday dinner, they sauntered along the roadway and, spying a good-natured peasant, hired him to drive them in his oxcart to their next stopping place.

Joking and laughing, the boys jogged along behind the sober, plodding team, calling friendly greetings to travelers on the roadside as they passed by.

Dusk was coming rapidly now and suddenly the driver stopped his oxen.

"I am a stranger in these parts, gentlemen," said he, nervously, "and from here, I do not know the way."

The boys looked at one another in alarm.

"My good man," began Frederic lamely, "nor do we know the road. Why not go straight ahead? Surely it will bring us to Ojcow."

Lurching along, the boys tried hard to see through the darkness that had fallen so rapidly, shutting out every ray of light.

Suddenly there was a tremendous splash and crunching of wheels on stone and, jumping from the cart, the boys found themselves struggling in the cold waters of the River Pradnik!

"Help! Help!" they called. But there was no one to hear them but the driver, who was struggling with his frightened beasts and could do nothing but sit in the cart and hold tight to the reins.

"This is a pretty mess! How now? Where to, comrades?" sounded from the stream.

Splashing and falling on the sharp boulders, the boys finally gave up trying to find the way and, standing in the swirling waters, called out with all their might. At last their cries were answered from the bank of the river.

"What will you have, gentlemen?" asked a faint voice.

"There has been an accident, sir," answered Frederic in relief. "And we cannot find our way to *Pan* Indyk, who has promised to put us up for the night."

"*Pan* Indyk! I know him well," answered the stranger. "Stay in the river and I will take you to him."

For half an hour in the darkness, they tried to follow his commands, but, in their wandering, stumbling over sharp stones and falling into icy, deep pools. At last, cold and exhausted, they reached the inn and, thanking their kind leader, crawled up to a small room under the eaves.

While the three other boys spread their wet clothing near the fire to dry, Frederic followed the wife of the innkeeper as she went off to get bedding. If only he could find a way to bind up his cold, aching feet, all would be well.

Spying some woolen nightcaps in an old chest, he turned eagerly to the plump little woman.

"Madame, if you will allow me, I should like to buy one of the headdresses."

In a moment he had torn it in two and, tying the pieces around his feet, crept into his hard bed on the floor, thinking how pleased his mother and sisters would be that he had warded off a bad cold!

On the very last day of July, the boys found themselves in the lovely old city of Vienna, the spire of the Cathedral of St. Stephen's shining cleanly into the heavens.

Walking through the narrow streets and beside the swiftly flowing Danube, Frederic felt as though he must be dreaming. On these very pathways had walked the merry-hearted Mozart, fun-loving Haydn, Schubert, the maker of sweet songs, and Beethoven, composer of mighty symphonies.

After happy days of sightseeing, Frederic at last took himself across the city to see the rascally Haslinger, well-known publisher of music.

"Ah, so you are the composer of the Variations that Elsner has sent to me," said he, rubbing his hands together and smiling nervously. "Then I must tell you that they will be printed in a very short time."

Frederic looked steadily at the man before him.

"I have been waiting a long time now, sir, and have been concerned at having no word from you."

"Yes, yes," agreed the business man hastily, watching from under his glasses the quiet, even-voiced young man. "But we are about to begin work now, I assure you."

After a moment's thought, he looked up suddenly.

"See here, young Chopin, you are not yet known to the people of Vienna. Why not give a concert so that your music can be heard?"

"But I have not seen a piano in these weeks of traveling, sir. I could not give a concert without a great deal of practice," answered Frederic.

Haslinger smiled. "That is simple enough. You will have three days and a piano, and one rehearsal with the orchestra."

Before Frederic could object, the plans were completed and notices sent at once throughout the city, announcing a concert by the gifted young Polish composer, Frederic Chopin.

And now a terror seized Frederic. To be prepared in so short a time was unthinkable! But shutting himself up in his room, he worked as he had never done before. And not once did his hands touch his own works or those numbers that he would play in the concert. Not once did he play anything but the works of the master, Bach.

Quietly the boys stole to his door but, hearing music whirling from the piano, left without a word.

"Poor Fritz!" sighed Hans. "He will be worn to the bone before the concert even begins."

The morning of the third day arrived and, leaving his room for the first time, Frederic went quickly to the hall for the rehearsal with the orchestra.

There were the men tuning their instruments, and taking his place at the piano, Frederic waited quietly as the parts of his rondo were passed out to the members.

In the front row sat Haslinger with Count Gallenberg, owner of the theater and writer of beautiful ballets.

"A newcomer to Vienna has plenty of difficulties in the musical world," explained the publisher.

"Too many," agreed the Count. "As to this young Pole, how will he play before an audience, think you?"

"Soon we shall see. There now, he is about to begin."

At a signal from the director, the men of the orchestra raised their instruments and began to play the music that Frederic had composed. But after a few bars they stopped, grumbling loudly.

"Young man," said their spokesman, "it is impossible to play this rondo of yours. The parts are so poorly written that we cannot read them."

Count Gallenberg left his place at once and approached the men.

"Come now, gentlemen," he pleaded, "surely it cannot be so bad. Do try again."

Still grumbling, the men took up their instruments, but with no better luck.

By this time, poor Frederic was in despair. His concert was sure to be a failure!

From the row of seats came the voice of Haslinger.

"Chopin, why not try the piece without the men?"

Too unhappy to speak, Frederic nodded his head and began. But instead of playing the rondo, he began to make a composition from a part of the opera he had heard only the night before. In beauty and strength his music rang out with such power that the men sat up, amazed.

"Enough! Enough!" cried Haslinger and the Count. "Save it, Chopin, for the performance tonight."

There were friendly cheers from the men of the orchestra and, in great relief, Frederic left the hall, to go on with his practicing until evening.

Darkness had begun to fall over the housetops when the boys gathered outside his door, not a little disturbed.

"Fritz! Fritz!" they called. "It is time that we were off to the hall."

His hands cold with excitement, Frederic followed the boys through the streets in silence. His test as a pianist was near at hand.

Just as they reached the concert hall, he turned to speak.

"Comrades," said he, "do not sit together this evening. Spread yourselves throughout the hall and listen with all your ears to what the people have to say. Then I will know what they really think about my playing."

A large audience was waiting as Frederic walked onto the stage, noble-looking in spotless waistcoat and well-brushed hair. Bowing with dignity to the scattered applause, he seated himself at the instrument and, squaring his shoulders and holding his head high, began his music.

Every tone was clear and rounded and the most difficult passages he played with such ease that the people were astonished. But Frederic had long forgotten them. A faraway look had come into his eyes and his face was pale as he keenly felt the music.

And now came his own composition made from a melody of an Austrian opera, so dear to the heart of the people of Vienna. A storm of applause greeted the first measure and at each new variation, composed as he went along, cries of delight and stamping on the floor rang out with such force

that Frederic could not hear his own playing.

"Bravos!" echoed through the hall as he finished the concert, and onto the stage flocked the people to shake the hand of the new young musician.

"A great success, Chopin!" cried Haslinger, his pale face glowing.

"And everyone is demanding more concerts," added Count Gallenberg. "We must plan another within a week, and a third, soon afterward."

Eagerly the boys pounced on their adored Frederic, telling him of the delight of the listeners seated around them.

"And when you played the Polish folk dances, the people near me began a dance on the benches!" added Franz.

What a celebration there was that evening, lasting on into the night, each of the boys vying with one another to do honor to their comrade. Frederic was far too excited to sleep and early the next morning, hurried into the street to buy a newspaper to learn more about his concert.

Rapidly his eyes searched the pages until he came to the article:

> "The gifted musician from Poland is like a beautiful young tree that stands free and full of fragrant blossoms and ripening fruits. His own compositions are the finest that Vienna has heard in many long months."

Waves of thankfulness swept over him. His music was a success! Perhaps he would be a famous pianist, after all, to be heard in many cities throughout the land.

But little did Frederic Chopin know how much more the whole wide world would come to know and love his music for the piano, telling in glorious melody of the beauty of his beloved homeland, Poland.

Isn't this a lovely bright waltz of Frederic Chopin's? You may like it so much that you will want to find the rest of the music and play all of it someday.

GRAND WALTZ
(TRACK 8)

www.ingramcontent.com/pod-product-compliance
Lightning Source LLC
LaVergne TN
LVHW061345060426
835512LV00012B/2567